RURAL LIFE I
DURING WORLD WAR TWO

RURAL LIFE IN RUNFOLD

DURING WORLD WAR TWO

AUTHOR & PUBLISHED by Bernard A. N. Green

ISBN 978-0-9576042-6-1

INTRODUCTION

The cover picture of Alf's Café at Runfold with me sitting in the Toll house garden was taken around 1936. This little book is partly about my life as a child growing up during the war years. I also relate true stories and poems.

I had great difficulty at school as I was accused of being difficult, a butterfly brain, stupid and a slow learner. The teachers did not understand dyslexia in those days. And as a result could be quite violent with pupils like me.

It was not until I was about twenty five years old that I was diagnosed as being dyslexic and not only that but I also suffer from dyscalculia (Difficulty calculating numbers). I was able to overcome these problems as I have explained in my books. Also in the book are poems about local people and events. All these stories are true and poems based on truth.

There are stories about the soldiers, waiting around this area for D Day and preparations for a possible German invasion. I write about German bombers and the devastating V1 Flying Bomb (THE DOODLE-BUG).

I have included stories of the activities I got up to as a child and the area I played in until after the war. The area that I covered as a child in the war years included The Sands village, and as far as Tilford, this area was full of soldiers on their way to fight or training for special missions.

These areas were not built up as they are now but were open woodlands and fields that I could walk across and had the occasional single wire fence depicting the boundary of the gardens of a very large house.

But those fences did not stop me from travelling in straight lines across the countryside. I spent days wandering between the army camps. Thinking about it now, I never had any trouble from dogs.

And nobody came looking for me or asked where I had been. Or where I had got food from.

CONTENTS

FAMILY

My grandfather A.E.A Green was working in the London Docks before the 2nd World War and had developed into a fine plumber and metal worker. He started working on submarines, perhaps because he was very small in stature, about five feet tall. Around 1934 he was asked to work in Portsmouth on submarines. As he now owned a newspaper shop in Tooting London which his wife managed; he used to cycle to Portsmouth on the A31 trunk road, leaving Monday morning and returning on Friday evening. This was a distance of about seventy miles. He would stop for a cup of tea at the Halfway House café and sweet shop in Runfold, Nr Farnham, Surrey. It was originally a Toll house and is still named The Toll House.

The café was aptly named, being halfway through the journey. However the original use of the house was The Toll House. When it was constructed over two hundred years ago it was to collect tolls from the travellers that wished to travel over the Hog's Back to Guildford. My grandfather obviously saw the potential and purchased this property and later in 1936 he sold it to my father.

I understand that my grandparents then managed the Jolly Farmer in Runfold and The Jolly Farmer at Blacknest near Bordon.

About 1940 they were running the Prince of Wales Pub at Hammer Bottom, Nr Haslemere at which time they separated and divorced in 1942. Kate Green opened The Green Library at 100 East Street, Farnham. This was a private lending library.

My grandfather became resident engineer at the Canadian War Veteran's hospital and Huron Camp which was situated opposite Bramshot Common on the A3 Nr Liphook, Hampshire. I observed first hand his skill in plumbing and metal work. He made baking tins with lids, kettles, pots and pans. He was particularly adept at making vases from gun shell cases. There is now a memorial park where the hospital stood in memory of the Canadian soldiers that died in WW2.

My father, having taken over the Toll House from my Grandfather in 1936, moved the café from the front room of the house into the garden shed. This shed or café leaned quite severely to the West after a Circus elephant decided to lean against it.

My father changed the name to Alf's Café. It was extremely popular with the soldiers that occupied all the big houses in the villages of Runfold and The Sands.

THE CAFÉ PHOTOGRAPH 1935

This photo I have estimated to have been taken around 1935. The car park had been created on top of a Victorian rubbish dump as the ground dropped away from the road. As a child I kept finding old glass bottles and pots when I dug holes in the garden.

The square building in the background was the village Post Office which was owned by Mr and Mrs Jerome.

The Café was originally a tea and sweet shop in the Toll House. There is an excellent photograph of the Toll house taken in 1895 on page 67 of the book The Lost Countryside by Chris Shepheard. It shows that it was popular with cyclists of the Farnham Road Club.

Hanging on the wall was the Cyclists' Touring Club sign which was later placed on the house front wall below my bedroom window. The article states that a purpose built teashop was built 30yrs later. That would make it 1925. However I think the garden shed was converted with a new outside toilet being built for the customers and it was also convenient for the Toll house occupants.

The overall dimensions were 19ft x 14ft. It was built with six upright pine trunks with the bark still on. The roof was corrugated iron sheets. The sides were assorted wooden panels.

Inside was an iron pot stove to keep the customers warm in winter. Tea was boiled in two kettles on a gas stove.

The depression in the roof and a slight leaning inwards of the wall was done by a circus elephant, in those days the elephants walked from town to town.

The little building at the back was the flush toilet. That was very modern as the Post Office only had an outside privy with a bucket. Bucket toilets were emptied by two men with a horse and cart and they used to come and empty once a week. . By around 1944 there was a huge telegraph pole right in front of the café door, it held about twelve cross bars to hold the multiple phone wires.

The house on the right (only the corner visible) was the residence of Lou Westbrook. He was foreman of the sandpit opposite the house operated by Ebeneazer Mears ltd. That was a wonderful Victorian name.

The face of this sandpit was at least 70ft (21metres high) if the face was vertical there was always the danger of a collapse and being buried. Lou Westbrook and his team worked with shovels. Starting at the top and creating a ledge about 18inches wide they could very easily move tons of sand which cascaded to the bottom. At the bottom a man could shovel 5tons of the loose sand onto a lorry in a very short amount of time, about half an hour. Not fast in today's world.

One day at 5pm I saw Lou step off the ledge and slide down the steep slope like a skier, holding the shovel behind him to help him balance. I thought that's good fun and we started doing it in the evenings using sticks for balance. We soon found we did not need the sticks as a tumble only meant landing in the huge soft pile of sand at the bottom. This could only be done in this pit due to the quality of the sand. There were no layers of ironstone and it did not have to be sieved for sale. Unfortunately Lou Westbrook was killed in the sandpit by a lorry when he was doing someone a favour after hours. His job was then taken over by Bill Walsh.

PICKFORDS PIT

Something that is not apparent is that behind the houses in Seale lane on the east of Blighton Lane, was that there had been a commercial

Sand-pit there. My mates and I used to go there to play. It had been dug below the water table at the far end and we made rafts to sail on it.

The sand face was about 40ft and we used to jump down into the wind-blown sand piled below. Until I landed on a railway sleeper buried in the soft sand. That was not soft. The pit had been opened in 1938 and closed in 1970. It was then infilled with rubbish and is now suitable for grazing animals.

Blighton lane was only about 8ft wide (244cm) in the 1940s. I was only 10yrs old when I watched a horse and cart come along the lane. It was piled very high with wheat straw from Sandy Farm. The straw was being pulled off both sides by the trees and bushes. I thought why pile so much on the cart only to get it pulled off.

Life was slower in those days.
The speed limit on this road is now 40mph.

THE TOLL HOUSE

The house adjoining the Café with the front door almost on the road was the Original Toll House for the section of the Old A31 up to the next Toll house about four miles over the Hogs Back. In the above photo the toll house is the nearest section painted white.

When I was a child there was a staircase to my room made of old doors. This made me very curious about the construction. Later I discovered that originally there was only a sleeping platform one third the size of the room and to get up onto it; you had to step on wooden pegs inserted in the eastern wall.

Originally the Chimney held a large coal fired cast iron range with an oven. The lower section of the building on the near side contained the wood fired copper pot for washing and boiling clothes. The toilet was a bucket. When my grandmother ran the downstairs room as a sweet shop and tea room, she had the fireplace blocked up. I unblocked it many years later. The toilet was still a bucket.

The drawing below shows the Toll House as it was originally built. It was single brickwork, no cavity. There was no foundation; the bricks were laid straight onto the sand (the famous Upper Greensand that builders loved). They used lime mortar, not cement. Despite all the great big steam engines, army tanks and huge Lorries trundling past on the A31 road only about 40inches (1metre) from the front door of the building. This part has not cracked, moved or sunk. Below I have drawn what it looked like as a Toll House. There was a small window by the side of the fireplace; this enabled the keeper to keep an eye on the traffic coming from the east direction. There was a similar window on the west.

There was a small outbuilding on the east side stretching from the chimney. This enabled a large wood fired copper pot in order to have the flue connected to the existing chimney. A low door was cut through the original building.
A toilet and wash basin was added years later in this little room. The copper was used for washing clothes and supplying hot water for our weekly bath. The 5ft tin bath was placed in front of the fire. It was babies first, father was last. It was the same water just topped up now and again with hot water.

The Cold room at the back of the house had a tiled roof. We went in there when the German bombers were dropping bombs on the Ammunition trucks being stored on the Tongham Railway. We heard stones rattling down the roof tiles. Two men named George F.W.Keen and George H. Leach were awarded the George Cross for detaching the burning trucks and shunting them away from the rest of the train. The ammunition was on the railway between Tongham and where the big roundabout at Farnham is now.

The line was opened on the 8th Oct 1849. It was for public transport and had twin tracks until1937 but then it was closed to the public and one track was kept for industrial use.

TOLL ROADS (WERE CALLED TURNPIKES)

The Guildford to Farnham Toll Road started with an Act of Parliament in 1758
Ref 31 Geo2c78
Distance 9 miles with two gates.
The incurred debt in 1838 was £2,215
The income in 1840 was £520

THE END OF THE TURNPIKES

Many turnpike trusts were wound up under General Acts of Parliament between 1873 and 1878. The transfer of resources and sale of assets to repay loans were supervised by the Local Government Board which acted as arbiter in the case of disputes. Toll-houses were sold, gates taken down and responsibility for the main roads passed to Highway Boards. Bond-holders were paid off with any residual funds,

If you are interested in building or architecture; our house was only about four feet from the road because it was built as a Toll House over 200 years ago. It was built with lime mortar and there are no footings, the bricks having being laid directly on to the sand. This sand is called Upper Greensand.

Despite all those tanks and heavy vehicles passing by there are no cracks in the old part of the building. Our house did not have electricity or mains toilet. We had coal fires and coal gas which was manufactured at the gas works in Farnham. The by-product of heating coal to create gas was coke. This was used extensively in this area to make roads and you can still see it built into walls.

Our house had brick and wood floors but some of my friends whose parents were farm workers living in tied cottages only had dirt floors and an outside tap for their water. Most neighbours had outdoor privies with buckets. The sewage was collected weekly by two men with a horse drawn cart with a metal tank on it. That was a very smelly job. But I noticed the men were always very happy.

THE TOLL HOUSE & POST OFFICE

The two photographs shown below of the Toll House and the Runfold Post Office were supplied by Geoff Lunn of the Sands Village. He is a successful wildlife photographer and gives talks on the subject.

Here is a photograph of the Toll House and the Post Office which I think was taken around 1895. The picture below I would guess at 1890 or perhaps a little earlier. I am looking at the walnut tree's growth rate.

The first mention of Runfold was in a map by a John Norden dated 1594 and spelt Runfolde.

THE OLD A31

The above photo is the old A31 at Runfold which was the main highway between Portsmouth and London and is part of the ancient trackway called The Pilgrim's Way. What a great time for cyclists, they had the road to themselves. The attractive building that is now The Jolly Farmer Public house did not exist when this photo was taken. It is now a Chinese restaurant. Note the high telephone pole with multiple cross bars to hold the many wires that cannot be seen in this photo.

HOP SACKS & MICE

Runfold and Farnham was a hop growing area. My bedroom was very cold because the walls were solid brickwork. Someone had put battens on the wall and stretched hop sacks over them. It was quite attractive with all the farmers' names and logo's printed on them. My mother was inventive and decided to wallpaper over them. She could not obtain glue because of the war, so she mixed flour and water as a paste to stick the wallpaper. This was fine for a while until the mice realized that it was a food source. So I had lots of little furry friends that would pop their heads out in a dozen of their favourite eating holes.

HOP FIELDS

This village of Runfold was a farming community. The main crop was hops for the brewing industry and nearly every acre in sight was covered by a network of poles and wires to support the vines. It was amusing to see the farm hands walking on stilts six feet high to tie the strings which would carry the vines. These strings had to be replaced every year. At the hop picking time the gypsies used to camp in the area to pick the hops by hand. I really enjoyed this period, the smell of bushels of hops, the noise and banter. Oh! How the farmers bartered about the quantity and condition too, for many leaves and sticks were buried under the hops in those huge wicker baskets to bulk them up.

The Rural Life Centre at Reeds Road, Tilford, Nr Farnham, Surrey has a display of authentic Gypsy caravans and every year hold a gypsy weekend. They will answer your questions and discuss the life that they have lost.

Runfold probably got its name from being a stopping place or fold for sheep being herded to London before vehicle transportation was used. There was a Pub, a Post Office and there were the petrol pumps owned by Mr Timperley who was also in charge of the Home Guard.
He was very much like Mr Mannering of the TV series Dad's Army. I informed him there was a grenade up the road, so he told the villagers to stand back and marched his troops up the road only to find it was a lemonade bottle with just the letters ADE showing.

MY GRENADE'S

Carbide lamps, or acetylene gas lamps, are simple lamps that produce and burn acetylene (C2H2) which is created by the reaction of calcium carbide (CaC2) with water (H2O). Acetylene gas lamps were used to illuminate buildings, lighthouse beacons, and as headlights on motor-cars and bicycles.
FROM WIKIPEDIA.

At an early age as I was mixing with soldiers I knew why Hand-Grenades exploded.

I had seen a lamp in the Post Office privy, and one day watched Mr Jerome put a white powder into it followed by a drop of water. This made a gas that produced a bright light. Being naughty and inventive at this young age I obtained some of that powder. Then I got a glass ink bottle (it was thick glass). Next I put a little powder in the ink bottle followed by a drop of water then screwed the metal lid tight on and threw it a short distance away. It exploded with glass flying in all directions, luckily none hit me.

Undeterred I then used this method to make Depth-Charges by dropping the ink bottle depth charges in ponds to sink my paper boats.

SPRING 1944, HOPPING

Spring is here and green
hop vines are climbing
seeking the warming sun
The strings tied in the spring
by men walking on 10ft stilts
to wires between the lines of poles

Poles fifteen feet high running
across the Surrey landscape
until they met the sky
Strings of Red Coir twine
made from coconut fibre in
the distant country of Ceylon

Harvest time three to four weeks
September to October. Land Army girls
took part, many married local men
Londoners came down on the train,
for them a working holiday.
Kids got fresh air and no school at all

The pickers, locals, gypsies,
women, old men and children
noisily crowded into the lanes
Workers pulled down the vines.
Women and old men picking
talking singing, children playing

Harvesting of hops, long gone
I miss the fresh smell of hops
picked by nimble fingers
Raw sore fingertips
from those rough vines that
hops use to climb the strings

Huge wicker baskets held the hops
A big basket contained a bushel,
the measure by which the farmer paid
He looked for tricks, leaves, sticks.
Tricks of the pickers to
bulk up their bushel baskets

It did not succeed
to bulk up their pay
at the end of the day
Workers were paid with Farmers Tokens
they could spend in the local shops.
Unless the old man had been in the pub

The baskets were placed on a cart
Hauled by two huge shire horses
to the local mill, hops to be dried
then pressed into a hessian bale
at least eight feet long
This system has now long gone

A world for which I did long,
but would not like to return,
for those days we were really poor.

SOLDIERS

All the local large village houses had been
requisitioned by the government and there were
many different regiments passing through on
their way to fight in the 2nd World War, British
and Canadian. They frequented the café as they
liked my father's home-made apple pies and
cakes especially the sweet pastry jam tarts. They
were full of sugar and this was a time of food
rationing, so that is how my father got involved
with the Black Market which I have written
about.

My favourites were the Canadians. They were
very generous with their food to me and I
watched America films in their special cinema
which was in the huge conservatory at the rear
of Homefields House at Whiteways-Corner. This
house with twenty-one rooms was purchased by
my father after the war and turned into a guest
house.

I have included a story about the Black Watch
Regiment and a Sergeant that caused me to

jump out of a window at Larchfield house which then caused my mother to fall for him. When the village was by-passed by a new A31 road it did not turn Runfold into a sleepy little village. It was then surrounded by Sand quarries excavating the famous Upper Greensand. After the sand was excavated they pits were then in-filled with rubbish.

During the war my father's café was very busy serving drivers that were travelling between London and Portsmouth. It was very interesting to me as a child. There were many Army vehicles, Bren-Gun carriers, Churchill and Sherman tanks rumbling and roaring through the village. There were Spitfires and Hurricane aircraft on large low loaders. There were even lorry's with steam engines hauling large loads, albeit very slowly.

THE BARRAGE BALLOON

A barrage balloon landed on the petrol pumps and the wires hanging under the balloon got tangled with the pumps. These balloons were used to stop enemy aircraft flying too low. But were also used to teach the Parachute Regiment solders by dropping them from a modified version. These were raised to 800ft on a winch. Many men were dropped by Static Line Parachute at the military playing fields at Queens Avenue Aldershot.

THE VILLAGE WITCH

The little lad looked at the house
It was me, a humble little mouse
I had heard my mother say, "She is a witch,"
or perhaps she said. "She is a bitch."

There was a dank smell, like cloth burning
Smouldering, smelly, stomach churning
With a wish, I threw a penny in her well
Is she a witch? No sound, it never fell

Tall towering trees, hanging over
No rabbits run, there is no clover
Timid tapping on the tremendous door
Opening abruptly, I fell down on the floor

Tock-tick, Tock-tick, the clock was Tocking?
Day, date dial, face quietly looking, mocking
The clock was angry with me, I could tell
It said Click clack, stared, and rang its bell

Stressing its size and importance Tack-Tock
Repeating itself Tack-Tock, I am a big clock

Gloom and doom, the old lady sits in the damp
Fluttering, guttering light from paraffin lamp

Sitting, sniffing, sewing away her final years
Lonely, bony, gaunt face but not crying tears
Will this witch throw me into her well?
Her bright blue eyes held me in her spell

Tea time is here, would you like some cake
She cackled, the scrumptious scones I did bake
She did me proud, fed me well, very nice tea
Was she trying to fatten me, then to eat me?

But that lady was good to me and kind
Sadly I cannot picture her face in my mind
She opened the huge door, to a fairy dell
Seen now, it is small, was I under her spell

She showed me round her secret garden glade
Heather, foxgloves, ferns, natural not man-made
Our conversation of that day has gone
but memories of that garden has shone

It has stayed with me, those quiet floral glades
Bright sunlight on leaves and soft sunlit shades
The wind wafted down golden pollen showers
Foxgloves fluttered their bell shaped flowers

Walking me to the gate she said, "thank you,
goodbye,"
Chaffinches chattered in her hedge as I passed
them by
Now my own garden is like hers, a Fairy glade
It has taken me over forty years to get it made

I believe that events as a child are deeply
implanted and in later years you can have
those wishes granted.

Note. I included this poem of mine to show how
my child's mind at that age and time was
thinking.

BILL THE BAKER

Bill Wilkinson was a strong, massive man
He lived in a village called Badshot Lea
In a of cottage of hand-made bricks, oak beams
This was where he owned the village bakery

Perhaps you thought the strongest man was the
blacksmith but flour sacks weighed two
hundred and twenty pounds or more
I believe the much stronger man was the baker
He had to carry those sacks to the upstairs floor

He had a huge mixing bowl which held a sack of
flour. To keep the dough warm, a wooden
proving bin, to keep it in.
The cottage loaves when proved, were placed in
the oven with a long oar like pole, sandwich
bread turned over in a tin

The oven, brick arched roof 2ft high 15ft long
10ft wide No gas, coal or electric was used, or oil
In the evening, baking done, he filled the oven
with faggots Silver Birch swishy branches, they
made brooms you'll recall

Early morning as he mixed the dough, with
paper he lit the wood, now very dry it burnt with
ferocious heat
Then with brush and mop he cleaned the floor of
ash. Scones cook first, then bread, cakes as it
cooled, rather neat!

The bread tins went in upside down this put
flecks of ash in the crust, rather nice
The proved loaf was turned over onto the paddle
then slid onto the bricks, a sprig of holly added
spice

I would collect twelve loaves of bread on my bike
Balanced on the handlebars and brakes

Chewing while pedalling, round the crispy
crusts. That birch ash was a better taste than
cornflakes

One day while watching him mix the dough
stripped to the waist, bent over the bin
Sweat running from all over his body
and dripping from his arms and chin

I was only eleven years of age, but I said
"Bill your sweat is going in the dough."
He laughed, but didn't bother to wipe his brow
"Yes, its salt, it makes for a better taste you
know."

Note. His name was William (Bill) Wilkinson; the
village of Badshot Lea is in Surrey, England.
The oven has been demolished but the house is
still there. Bill called the bundles of Birch tree
bundles 'faggots' but others have called them
'Bavins'.

After the Homefields Guest House at Whiteways
Corner burnt down in the 1950s my father
purchased the land behind the Post Office and
built a new Alf's Café. In later years I learnt to
be a baker from Bill when I was demobbed from
the Royal Engineers Regt. I then opened a

bakery in my father's café. In later years I purchased the Café from my father.

The Runfold Bakery and the village farm was owned by Mr Tice and consisted of 252 acres arable, 41 acres under hops with poles and wires and 96 acres of grass. The bakery which had a brick oven fired (heated) by burning birch tree tops in the oven itself. The oven has now gone.

THE BLACK MARKET

At the rear of our Toll House was a large galvanized iron garage. This is where our coal was kept. Of course it was on ration because of the war but we had a big pile of it. I would guess that there was half a ton. One summer night at about midnight my father awoke me from a deep sleep. He told me to get dressed. "What have I done?" I asked. He only replied "Come down-stairs." In the kitchen he was lighting a paraffin lamp. I waited for the punishment without knowing what I had done to deserve it. "Follow me." I followed him into the dark garage fearful of what he was going to do. He put the lamp down and handed me a shovel and said, "Move that coal from there to over there." With that he walked back into the house leaving me alone to shovel the coal.

I was relieved to be left alone after anticipating a whacking with a swishy stick. I started shovelling the coal. Within a few seconds I was surrounded by hundreds of wasps. I had seen plenty of them before in the Café; buzzing around the apple and jam tarts. I continued shovelling the coal with the wasps buzzing around angrily, I had learnt not to swat at them Then I found the reason. Sugar, bags and bags of it, each over one hundred weight and the wasps had found it and had burrowed into one of the bags.

Now I understood why I was told to move the coal. My father was terrified of being stung. I had seen him swatting at them and running away when they attacked him. Better for me to get stung for I was young, perhaps he was highly allergic to stings, I do not know. He did not even check on my progress. When I had uncovered all the bags I went into the house, reported to him and went to bed.

Note. Sugar ration was 8oz per person per week until 1953.

COAL

Coal was rationed at 50cwt (2540kg) per year per family from July 1941 until 1958. Remember that houses were heated by coal fires. 15/1/1944 The MINISTRY OF FUEL AND POWER issued an advertisement stating, '5lb. of Coal saved in one day by 40,000 homes will provide enough fuel to build a Churchill Tank. Save fuel for battle.'

There was a ton in our garage.

MILK

Do you remember the milk bottles that had cardboard tops with perforated round holes in the middle? At school you pushed your straw through the hole or your little finger to hook the lid off to drink from the bottle. Ok, if you remember this then you are very, very old. Why do I tell you this? Because that was my daily job!

The milkman dropped off crates of milk while he had his breakfast, free of charge I suppose. With my tiny fingers I popped off all the lids from the full cream milk and then my father would tip out half of the cream and add water. I then had to put new caps on; it was a production line which produced extra bottles of milk. N.B. Milk was rationed at 3 pints per adult per week. The café needed milk.

LONG HILL, SANDS VILLAGE

This next story took place as the sun was setting and my father took me for a ride in his Morris Eight car. These trips were very exciting. He was always working so I never had a holiday with my dad. He drove about two miles and parked in a narrow unmade road bounded by pine trees. It was a plantation of pines, the trees were close together. We were about one hundred yards in from the road. After sitting there in silence for a while an army lorry came along and backed up to dad's car. Without a word two soldiers started putting great lumps of meat into the car. There were huge cow's legs and ribs. I had never seen so much meat.

No sooner than the doors were shut when an Army jeep came up the road with soldiers that had big red hats on. On seeing the lorry they started to drive up behind it. They could not get past because of the trees. My father jumped into the car and drove off. I thought he cannot go far but I was wrong because the track ran for a mile and came out onto another road opposite a pub called The Donkey at Elstead, within a short time we were home.

There are a number of beautiful houses in those woods now and you cannot drive right through now.

Quite a funny way to purchase beef, but there was a war on. Meat was rationed from 8/1/1940 until 4/7/1954. One person's weekly ration was equivalent to 2oz. of minced beef. Father made wonderful meat pies; also apple and jam tart for the soldiers.

This track, which in the war only led to an abandoned sanatorium, is now called Long Hill in the village of Sands. According to further information the sanatorium closed in 1943. So I must have been between 9 to 10yrs old.

The sanatorium had a private electricity plant. It was abandoned. I found that the glass tubes in the acid vats that were about 14inches long made excellent peashooters. So I washed them thoroughly and sold them at school.

CHARLIE BACKHURST

Charlie or Charles Backhurst, lived in Badshot, Surrey UK. He was a friend of my father and was what I would describe as a countryman. He was self-employed as hedge trimmer, grass cutter, anything that kept him out in the open air.

After 1942 Charlie started taking me out with him to collect moss. Most people think, if you stand still too long, you will collect moss. It was quite hard work. Why collect it? All the florists wanted it for wreaths and floral arrangements they also wanted it dewy fresh. I vividly remember the first time out with him, He collected me before the sun rose and drove out into the countryside. I never ever knew where I was but it was always remote, no cars, houses or people. It was peaceful, heavenly with the sun starting to peep through the woodland and the birds waking each other with their singing. There were red squirrels then. I was handed a small rake and a sack, the type of sack used for Army sandbags. Within the woods there were natural clearings that were maintained by the rabbits and deer. Here was the thick moss, wet with the morning dew. He showed me how to rake the moss and at the same time avoid collecting sticks, stones brambles or fir cones. I amassed a tangle of beautiful green moss and start to fill the sacks. This continued for hours until Charlie got out jam and cheese sandwiches, to me this was absolute bliss.

After breakfast he got a 410 shotgun out of the pickup then after showing me how to walk quietly he would go shooting rabbits. He constantly surprised me by his ability to jump on top of a hare, he would be walking through the grass and suddenly jump sideways into a clump of grass then pick up a stunned hare that had been hiding there.
We would come round a corner and find a group of rabbits eating or socializing and he would fire. With these small calibre guns, the range could be 75ft (20 metres). Eventually he gave me a gun. I could not shoot if they were too close and I could look into their eyes.

We would gut and skin the rabbits straight away as it is easier to do when they are freshly killed. This was long before a terrible disease called Mixi (Myxomatosis) effected the rabbit population and I stopped eating wild rabbit. Now and again we would net rabbits. I had gone out with other people that caught rabbits using ferrets but found it to be laborious as you have to ensure that you cover every escape hole with a small net pegged down, then put your ferret down the hole. Ferrets have a very bad smell, it is really obnoxious and they tend to bite with teeth that can go right through your finger. Sometimes the ferret catches a rabbit down in the burrow and stays there to eat and then have a nap. So then you have to dig him out, but that is only if you love your ferret enough.

Netting is different, at midday when the bunnies had gone down the burrows to snooze away the hot afternoon. Charlie and I would lay a net that was about 150 yards long (40m) and 24inches (61 cm) high. It was placed along the edge of a field adjoining a wood, a favourite place was at the back of Inglewood House between the villages of Runfold and The Sands. The net had to be propped up with sticks which we snapped off the hedge rows, having done that, we departed for the rest of the day and returned to the opposite side of the field when it was quite dark. I would be handed a box of matches and with both of us rattling the matches in the box walked steadily across the field towards the net.

This noise did not create a panic in the rabbits and they headed for home in a fast but orderly fashion and dozens hit the net which collapsed on top of them. It was then necessary to pick them up by the legs and chop their neck with the edge of the hand to kill them, a rabbit punch. These rabbits were all in the butchers next morning.

The 410 shotguns were called poachers guns because they were very light in weight and folded up at the junction of the barrel and the wooden stock. On firing they were relatively quiet with the noise not carrying very far. If you wished to conceal the gun you hooked a ring of cord around the middle of the folded gun then hung it over the shoulder, the gun would then hang under the arm below a coat or jacket without any outward sign it was there.

There was another way of shooting rabbits called Lamping, but I did not like it because the rabbit just sits in the beam of the powerful torch light and is such an easy target, another reason is I did not like eating shotgun pellets,
The netting method collected healthy animals with no lead in them.

THE LANCHESTER CAR

In 1946 my father won a huge six cylinder Lanchester car by a bet on the horse called Lovely Cottage in the Grand National. The car had a glass division and speaker tubes for the chauffeur. He took all the family to Ilfracombe in Devon, the baby, pram and the girl next door called Avril who was the daughter of Lou Westbrook, who was the foreman of Ebenezer Mears sandpit. A distance of 380 miles, and this was when petrol was still strictly rationed. A policeman stopped us but on seeing the baby, and children, said "Go on your way, you have enough problems."

About five miles out of Ilfracombe the carburettor played up so my father laid me in-between the bonnet and the front mudguard to tickle the carburettor until we arrived at the hotel. This car probably did 15 mpg. We had jerry cans on the luggage rack at the back and inside the car. He left us there for a week at a hotel owned by my father's friend, a Mr Tony Carrol.

What would the child welfare people think of that if someone was caught putting their child on the bonnet of their car?

PETROL RATIONING

Petrol was rationed from 1939 to May 1950.

The following was an article in the Farnham Herald. 22/1/1944. Bear in mind that Mr Chitty was only about three miles from his place of work.

PETROL USED FOR WRONG PURPOSE.

Mr M. J. Chitty was summoned and fined 15 Shillings (which I think was equal to half a week's pay in those days.) for using Motor fuel acquired for coupons other than that to which the coupons were issued. Police asked why he was travelling in the wrong direction. The defendant said he thought he was allowed to travel to get spare parts for the vehicle.

It was now 1943; I was nine and a half years old. I knew about the war, for we had troops stationed in requisitioned large Victorian houses which abounded in this area. I had heard the German bombers coming over with their engines synchronized in cruise mode making a sound like wow-wow-wow. This was when they bombed the railway line which ran from Farnham to Tongham upon which stood ammunition trucks. I wonder how they knew they were there.

THE DOODLEBUG

I was ten years of age and exercising my father's racing grey-hound. He was called VIM. I had left the village of Runfold and was heading south across some high open ground when I heard a peculiar sound. I interpret this noise as Brrr-Brrr-Brrr. This intermittent pulse was coming from an aircraft heading straight towards me. All I could see was a round nose and thin wings, as I was a keen aircraft spotter I knew that this was no ordinary plane. It was not very high above the tree tops. It was less than half a mile away. I then realized with alarm that this was a V1, or Doodlebug as the Londoners called it.

The first V1 dropped on England on 13/6/1944 and by the 16th of June, seventy three had hit London. It was now August that same year. This one was heading straight for Aldershot, the Home of the British Army three miles behind me, whether this V1 was aimed at Aldershot or the RAF at Farnborough directly behind Aldershot, nobody will know. When it ran out of the predetermined fuel or the wind driven milometer cut the engine. This is the moment it happened, silence for about five seconds as it dropped behind the trees. Apparently the blast could radiate two miles but I was protected by the trees. There was an enormous bang, a column of dirt, debris, wood and bricks rose hundreds of feet up into the air.

Our dog Vim bolted towards the explosion; I remember thinking that this was very odd. I would be in trouble if I lost my father's racing greyhound.

He was so fast that my father used to put elastic bands round his toes to slow him down in order to raise the Bookies betting odds for the next big race at Tongham Dog Track. I ran after him through the woods and gardens of Inglewood, a large Victorian house that had been requisitioned by the Army, but was now empty. Coming out of the trees, there in front of me were the remains of Sandy farm which had been a four bed-roomed house with a yard which had consisted of a cattle shed, a milking parlour and stables. On the open side had been a large haystack. All that was left was a pile of rubble and a small ironstone wall beside the road. The ironstone wall is still there.

I ran on top of the rubble, calling out "VIM-VIM-VIM". But he was nowhere to be seen, I was terrified of losing him. My father would have been very hard on me. I stood there on top of the rubble looking at the devastation.

The rubble was moving like a jelly, wobbling, pulsating. Looking down I could see a massive amount of blood oozing up between the brick rubble, broken timbers and hay. There was a terrible sweet sickly smell. I realized that the cows had been in the yard for milking, now all dead or dying beneath my feet. Strangely it did not occur to me at all that there might be people there under my feet.

I ran off the heap of rubble calling VIM. I now wonder if the people under the rubble were still conscious, did they think the child's voice was an angel calling or perhaps the Devils work. I never saw any person on the way there, on the farm or going home. I now know that there were five people under the rubble; three died the others were badly injured.

Apparently it took a considerable time for rescue services to turn up. Also there was nothing in the papers except that a V1 landed in the countryside, further stating there was no major damage. This was part of the propaganda war to stop the enemy knowing the true damage caused.

On arriving home there was the dog, unharmed. Now another strange thing that I cannot explain, I never ever spoke to anyone about this until writing this now. There must be some psychological reason for this. Perhaps that is why some war veterans never want to talk about their experiences?

All the large houses in this area were requisitioned by the army and perhaps all the troops had gone off to fight. Just a few hundred yards away was a beautiful house in the trees called The Spinney. The Army Officers had used this as their accommodation and headquarters. A lot of guns, trucks and tanks had been stored under the trees in The Sands prior to this Doodlebug dropping. I believe the road named Compton Way was built by soldiers for this purpose. I had seen arms and ammunition all hidden in the trees along the side of this road. This road is now full of the most beautiful houses in the Farnham area lining each side of this twisting undulating road.

The V1 was most probably launched in France. It carried about 680 litres of fuel and took half an hour to get here at 650 km an hour. The explosive carried was 1,870 lbs of Amatol 39. The blast could be felt two miles away. For those military enthusiasts, the farm co-ordinates are 51 deg 12' 48.81N, 0 deg 44' 45.17W Elevation 93 metres.

On the 18/11/2010 I visited the fabulous Surrey History Centre in Woking and found an article printed in The Farnham Herald newspaper of 12/8/1944. It reported, Flying Bomb Deaths. The farmer, together with Mr Fred Kirk, Mrs Davis and her 13 year old daughter, Doreen, Mr Norman kirk and residents of some cottages attached to the farm were seriously injured and taken to hospital. The farmer's wife Mrs Ellen Martin and daughter Winifred Kirk who were in the farmhouse were killed instantly. Under the rubble that I had been standing on was the farmer Mr Kirk, Mrs Davis and her daughter Doreen, they were severely injured. All the cows and poultry were killed. This flying bomb was the first type of pilotless plane known as a German flying bomb, V1, Doodlebug as Londoners called them.

Of all the square miles of open countryside it landed smack in the middle of this little farm. Another three miles and it would have been in Aldershot. The farm was totally demolished but for the Ironstone wall. That is still visible and fronts onto the Sands road. Sandy farm has

been completely rebuilt and is now called Sandy
Farm Business Centre.
I wrote a poem about my feelings. It is below.

Brr-Brr THE DOODLEBUG

Brrr-Brrr-Brrr
Listen to that noise, it's a Doodlebug, I hear

Brrr-Brrr-Brrr
That is a German Pilot-less drone, it's near

Brrr-Brrr-Brrr
Waiting for the noise to stop, I feel the fear

Brrr-Brrr-Brrr
Half ton of explosive in the nose, coming here

Brrr-Brrr-Brrr
First Pulse jet, engine on top, at the rear

Brrr-Brrr-Brrr
It is passing over us, we are safe. Cheer

Brrr-Brrr-Brrr
Fuel measured for distance, aimed straight here

Brrr-Bop-Bop-Pop then silence
Engine has stopped; it starts to stall, to veer

Ten seconds silence as it fall's, shed a tear
Boom, debris fills the sky.
A whole family disappear. It's war, oh dear.

REQUISITIONED HOUSES

Several large houses in the villages of Runfold
and The Sands were requisitioned by the Army
during the Second World War; Homefields,
which was at Whiteways Corner, Runfold, was
demolished and the site is now a sandpit
operated by a company called Chambers.
Woodlands and Sandhurst, are on the A31 near
Runfold. Inglefield and the Spinney are in the
Sands village. Runfold Manor just round
Whiteways corner was for the Higher ranking
officer's use.

The Spinney was and is a splendid example of
Art Nouveau/Art Deco style with beautiful Oak
floors, doors and fittings. It was fitting that the
officers used this house as their headquarters
and I was not able to enter it until the Army
disappeared to go to D-Day. My friends and I
walked around this wonderful house that had
radiators and every modern convenience. Bear
in mind that the house I lived in had an outside

toilet and one of my friends lived in a house with dirt floors and no inside toilet or bathroom.

There was a chandelier hanging in the main lounge on the west side of the house and the windows had large oak window sills.
I had seen a film with the swashbuckling Errol Flynn swinging on a chandelier to fight his enemies so I thought I would try it.

I dived off the window sill and grabbed the brass ring of the chandelier only for the whole thing to become detached from the ceiling and I and the brass and the glass crystals came crashing to the floor. I cannot drive past this house without a feeling of guilt.

DEFENSIVE MEASURES

Something that people are not aware of is that during the war, between the Hogs Back Hotel and Guildford there were huge concrete pillars. They were approximately 6metres high and 1metre wide. These were probably 100metres apart and either side of the old A31. I have had to guess the dimensions as I was between the age of 8 to 11yrs old when I saw them. They were to stop enemy aircraft or gliders landing but there were plenty of open fields close by.

My father used to drive up onto the Hogs Back on some nights and we would watch the German bombs exploding in London and fires raging. Occasionally he did some bomb damage clearing with a small lorry.

Towards the end of the war I saw a Bomber had crash landed on the Hogs back without any apparent damage. I am sure that it was an Avro Lancaster as it had a square fuselage. I believe it must have landed on the strip of grass west of the current car park and café. Incidentally there were no trees either side of the road then.

GUN POSITIONS (PILLBOXES)

These were commonly called Pillboxes. The first one I will describe is at Whiteways corner on the old A31 in Runfold. A lot of young people will not be aware of its existence as it is built below the level of the road and hidden by trees and vegetation. It is on the north side of the road 50 metres past the 40mph sign. It is built of brick and the walls are 2ft thick.

There are seven loopholes which is the term for little holes for shooting through. One of these looks straight up the road coming down from the Hogs Back. Another looks at Whiteways Corner. There were two pillboxes on the high ground south of the road but they have disappeared into the Sand pits. Rifles and machine guns (Bren Guns) could be used in this position. I shudder to think of the effect on undefended ears.

There were a great number of these pillboxes built across the south of England. They seem to follow a line south of the Hogs Back. There are two gun posts at the entrance to the ruins of Waverley Abbey. The one by the gate was for a large field gun which covered the valley. It therefore has a very large entrance at the rear and a very wide gun port.
I saw this as a child and it was built to look like a house. It was built in 1940 as one of the gun ports has that year embedded in the concrete. There are numerous pillboxes in this area and if you want to know more then look on the internet at Exploring Surrey's Past, Surrey's Pillboxes.

WAVERLEY ABBEY FIELD GUN POST

In the photograph below, this is the view through the gun port from inside the building where the gun could fire right across to the river Wey. There were other gun positions in this valley and it was all designed as a 'Killing Field'. A short distance away in the field to the south is a pillbox for the use of rifles or machine guns. This position could provide covering fire for the large rear entrance of the field gun position.

In Tilford village by the bridge and ford there is an almost identical example of the layout. If you stand on the bridge and look to the north side, they are clearly visible.

The one close to the bridge is for the Field gun which faced up the valley. I found this strange as I know there are other pill boxes up the valley. There were two pillboxes close by on the south side of the bridge. There was another pillbox on the other side of the river behind the Public house.

The very thick concrete wall you can see was to protect the wide rear entrance. A short distance away is the pillbox which could provide covering fire and also covers the bridge and up the valley. Apparently the large number of pillboxes in the valley along the River Wey was designed as 'Killing Fields' and what I have shown is just a tiny part of the scheme to stop any German invasion on the south side of the Hogs Back.

This was all part of The Home Counties Stop Line which was a small part of The GHQ STOP LINE.

THE TILFORD PILL BOXES

The two large square concrete blocks left in the field look very heavy? They were most probably used to block the ford, (the river crossing beside the bridge). It would have needed a substantial mobile crane to move those blocks! But there were plenty of the big Lorries around for moving broken down tanks. Where they are placed at the moment would have been in the firing line of the field gun.

Nature has given both pillboxes very attractive Ivy hats.

I have passed through Elstead many times and visited the pub called The Woolpack and only recently did I see the loopholes in the high stone wall opposite the pub which covers every road.

If you would like further information The
ELSTEAD GHQ LINE is an interesting Pillbox
study group website.

The Tilford Bridge can be seen in the
background.

BOTANY HILL, THE SANDS

In the 2nd World War, the Canadian Army were based in this area and built a concrete road known as Compton Way, The Sands village where they stored Tanks and Guns hidden under the trees, waiting for 'D' Day.

In the village of The Sands I own some land north of Botany Hill road, on this site the army were also waiting for D-day and there was an anti-tank trench which can still be seen. It was excavated east to west. At the bottom north-east corner of the estate are the footings and remains of the kitchens that were cooking for the troops.

Following the war there were two Land Army girls living in a two room wooden hut at the top of the estate. The Concrete footings are still there. Unfortunately in 1972 my son aged 12yrs climbed on the roof and it collapsed.

THE SANDS VILLAGE CIRCA 1909

In the picture below the land in the foreground had been planted with Christmas trees.

The large old house 2nd from the right had been a public house. It had a well on the east side. The current owners think the original building was built between 1865 and 1871.

The row of almost identical houses in the background were built in 1909. They were intended to make the Sands a show village.

Each one had a separate purpose. One was for a blacksmith, another for a shop, but the very clever idea was that the end house on the right of the picture was to be a commercial laundry.

The whole of the house, both bottom and top floor was designed to enable the washing and ironing laundry. A very unusual feature was that all the rainwater from the roofs of all the other buildings was channelled to this house to use in conjunction with tap water in order to save money. The project did not progress further due to the war.

ANTI-TANK TRENCH

There was an anti-tank trench dug that was right across the Hogs Back. As a child I saw the scar cutting across the countryside changing colour from the yellow sands of the Sands and Runfold villages to the white of the chalk on the Hogs back. Where it started and where it ended I did not know. But I was told recently that it started at Manor farm in Tongham and finished north of Farnham.

A few years ago I saw a ditch in my land in the sands. I was puzzled as water drains away quickly in the sandy soil. I dug a trench across it to discover why it was there. It was the anti-tank trench. But seriously it might have stopped a lorry, jeep or perhaps a Bren Gun Carrier but not a German Panzer tank.

On the south Side it was originally about 5ft high and I could still see the Wattle coppicing hurdles used to support the soil. They were approximately 5ft high and 6ft long. The ditch was V shaped with the south side being almost vertical. The north side sloped away with the excavated soil on the north side.

I have taken a photograph, shown below of what remains to be seen. The army was camped to the left of this area. I have found knives and forks with army numbers on them and rusted army tools used for repairing tanks.

I have been told the Canadian soldiers were stationed near Hankley Common. In 1943 they constructed a copy of something called THE ATLANTIC WALL. They then tried various methods and types of explosives to create gaps in it. It was all connected to Operation Overlord in France 1944.

WATTLE FENCING

Wattle and Hazel fencing was and still is coppiced. Meaning the branches are cut from new growth and therefore the roots provide new growth each year.

There was a Pillbox on the high land opposite the western end of Botany Hill, but it is hidden or demolished. It faced straight up Botany hill.

THE AMMUNITION CAVE

Actually it was a tunnel dug into the hard sand hillside in Camp hill, Waverley Lane. My friend and I found it when the army were still there. We couldn't get too close to it until they left for D day. The entrance was opposite the house that adjoins the footpath that leads to Mother Ludlum's cave, which was one of our haunts.

We both ventured inside, we could see a dim light, after about fifty metres the tunnel turned sharp right and a smaller doorway came out onto the Waverly road about one hundred metres from the corner with Camp hill. It had been dug like a coal mine; it was about eight feet wide and 6ft high with timber supports every few feet.
It had been used to store boxes of ammunitions for the infantry and the Army tanks that had been hidden in the trees surrounding the local area. Soon after our visit we found that the entrance and exit had been blown up. The exit is not at all visible but where the entrance was the hillside has an indentation which is difficult to show in a photograph.

PRISONERS OF WAR

After D-Day there were Italian prisoners of war in Homefields house, I don't say held because there were no guards. Then later there were a few Germans prisoners. Many of the Italians stayed in the area and became successful in business.

When my father purchased Homefields and turned it into a hotel one of the Germans stayed and worked for him for a while. I think his name was Gunter Fisher, it sounded like 'Kinter'. When he returned to Germany he wrote to my sister for a while until he found himself on the wrong side of the Berlin wall with the Russians and the letters were stopped.

Larchfield house was opposite Alf's Café in Runfold and was the house I mention in THE BLACK WATCH story. After the soldiers it housed the Land Army girls. It was then managed by Mr & Mrs Auge. Then the house was sold to a mining company called Ebenezer Mears. The house was eventually demolished to extract the sand below it. It has now been completely filled with rubbish and topped with soil and is suitable for grazing.

ADULTS ARE ODD

My father, taught me to go and get, to fetch
He'd say, go to the field, pull carrots and veg
Down the lane and get the spuds,
I should say potatoes, excuse me
Those strawberries up the road
go and pick a packet for tea
That cherry orchard, they are red, time to collect
I recollect, he said cherries tonight, don't forget
A policeman nabs me, pulls me home by me ear
I'm full of fear. Say's, "Your lad was scrumping
cherries, clip 'is ear."
I'm smacked, by me dad. Plod departs;
Justice has been done. I've been naughty
Strange how adults think, I was whacked for
something that me father taught me?

Note. Scrumping, meant to steal fruit from
orchards.

THE POPULATION CHART

In 1946 a chart was shown to the class at East
Street School predicting the growth pattern for
the world population. It looked like what we
now know looks like an atomic mushroom
cloud. I was then 12 years old. The sustainable

level of human occupation is about 2 billion. There are now about 7 Billion.

An Asteroid crashing into earth is required to change all that. A natural pandemic or perhaps it will be a chemical or biological war that will decimate the population. I wrote the following poem in 2012.

THE POPULATION EXPLOSION

Earth has a thin veneer, not all of it habitable
Only part of its mass is productive and liveable
That can provide safe shelter, food and water
All species eventually outgrow their space
And that applies to the human race
Politics call for greater growth
It's too late for our species
Living in rubbish, faeces
Far too many people
It's unsustainable
And unstoppable
Armageddon
Is soon
BOOM
FIN

B.A.N.Green.

UNKNOWN DANGERS

I was ten years of age, my friend Roy Jarvis and I had such a wonderful playground, miles of countryside. Barracks full of soldiers waiting for D Day, the woods were full of tanks and vehicles. The soldiers delighted in showing us to climb out of third floor windows to descend on knotted ropes. There was no "Elf & Safety" here; we even tried some of their assault courses.

GINGER BEER

One day we were at the rear of Larchfield in Runfold. This was one of the Victorian houses which had been taken over by the Army, when we found cases of Ginger beer. Well they were Ginger beer bottles, and if you are old enough you will remember those brown stone bottles with crimped metal caps. These were Ginger beer bottles but they did not have any writing on them. We both liked this drink so we took four bottles each and tried to open them, we knocked the crimped lids on trees to try and dislodge them. But without an opener we could not.

In exasperation we threw them into a quarry. To our utter astonishment when they broke there was white smoke and fire.

Later we found out that they were cheaply manufactured phosphorous grenades. Phosphorous will burn through skin and bone. We were very lucky boys.

Both of us were adventurous and I suppose not under parental control because Roy's father was fighting in the war and my parents were too busy working in their café. The quarries I mentioned were for digging the excellent sharp sand that runs parallel to the A31 road. There was a depth of seventy feet before you hit the water table.

THE WELL

Roy and I walked into a group of derelict buildings, they used to make sand paper sheets there, and it might surprise you to know that it was not for rubbing down woodwork but to put in the bottom of the popular canary or budgerigar cages to catch the droppings. This was an interesting and profitable way to sell sand. Among the debris of a collapsed wooden building we discovered a hinged lid in the ground and opened it. It was a well we dropped stones and after a long interval heard "splosh";

I noticed iron hoops hammered into the brickwork joints of the brick lining. We decided to investigate. I went down first, and Roy followed; down and down making sure that we held on with both hands before stepping on the next rung. I stopped to look up, it was pitch dark and the entrance above looked like a distant star, we never had a torch. Then Roy stood on my fingers. Taking that hand away with a yelp, at the same time I stepped down quickly, the next rung broke away, it was fortunate the rung that I held on to did not break. We climbed out; I think that well was over sixty feet deep. No one knew where we were, had we fallen or the well collapsed. It makes me shiver now.

THE LAUNDRY

Not deterred by this near calamity our next adventure was a tall chimney stack that we could see from our East Street School playground in Farnham Surrey. One lunch time we trotted out of school to the chimney which was at the rear of a laundry in the Guildford road. We did not understand the connection!

There was a steel hatch, we opened it and climbed in and it was enormous, like a big black cave, a lot of soot and there were rungs going up inside. We both wanted to get to the top and look down at our school, but it was very dirty, sooty and harder than expected to climb. We gave up. Retreated happy and in a very grubby state to school. What we did not know then was that; had the laundry workers' lunch hour finished while we were in the chimney, they would have fired up the gas fire boilers. Our goose would have been cooked.

Note. My childhood friends Roy Jarvis and Desmond Jarvis lived in Flint Cottages, on the A31 road in Runfold. They had a sister called Delia.

Until the war ended I did not see Mr Jarvis as he was a prisoner of war in a German Stalag Camp. He was terribly thin when he came home.

TOYS

Only the other day my son asked me what toys did I have as a child. The answer was none, but I had a home-made bow and arrows, a home-made catapult. Home-made pea-shooter.

And best of all was home-made Go-cart which I made from old pram wheels and a plank of wood, a bolt to hold the steering board, and string to steer with. I used to start my journey at the high point of Crooksbury Hill and get to the corner where the footpath goes to Runfold. A distance of about 1.5 Km. I did not meet any cars; people did not have cars in those days.

There was a Yellow Bus service which started in 1928. It travelled between Guildford and Farnham seven times a day. I did not meet it as I came down Crooksbury road and the bus travelled on the Sands road past the Golf club. He would have seen me coming when he or she stopped at the T junction.

Children travelled free! The charge for an adult from Farnham to the Sands crossroads was four and a half pence. But my mother still walked to Farnham and back to save money. The really nice thing was that the driver would drop you off at your house if it was on the route.
The Yellow bus service started in 1938 with Dennis Pike buses that had 20seats. By 1945 they had 6 utility buses. The end of the friendly Yellow Bus Service was in 1958 when it was purchased by another Bus Company.

EAST STREET SCHOOL, FARNHAM 1946

The teacher sharpened his pencil
I admired his dexterity, his style
Now I know it was displacement activity

He used a small silver penknife
Staccato movements of his flicking hand
It was show time, a display, an Art Form

The girls got cuddles, and extra tuition
Boys got short thrift, and punched on the head
His fist had three gold rings, one like twisted rope

I'm dyslexic I got hit a lot, Roy got hit very hard
It started his epileptic fits, Revengeful thoughts
when I grow up. He died, a heart attack.

HEATH END SECONDARY SCHOOL

I thought I was going to leave school when I was
14 years of age. Just before I left school I was
told it was now to be 15yrs of age. I was told I
had to do another year and was being sent to a
school that had just been built.You will
understand why I hated school.It was because o
the teacher's violence at East Street School. A

woman teacher had used a horse whip to hit me with as well as being punched on the side of my head many times by a male teacher. He had three large gold rings like knuckledusters.

The new school was called Heath End Secondary Modern School which is on the outskirts of Aldershot. When all the new students arrived at this school the builders were still there. I noticed straight away the difference in procedures. At East Street we would stay in the same classroom and the teachers would know you all personally, too personally my view.
At Heath End Secondary School we walked into the first class and a roll call was taken. After the first lesson and all subsequent lessons the students moved from class to class and the teachers stayed put.

After an incident with a maths teacher who said I was cheating because I solved a maths question without the traditional system of working and writing out the equation. I decided to register at the very first class and then slide off for the rest of the day, nearly every day.

Occasionally I got pressganged into fixing the coat hangers into the cloakrooms and also spent some time digging a fishpond for the school which seemed the headmasters dream project. It is only last week I met an ex pupil that was working on that pond with me and made me think about it. I only ever played one game of football at this school and gave up after heading the ball. It was a heavy leather ball and the leather lacing cut my forehead, but for some reason I was voted Captain of Cobbett House. I did not do much to earn the title.

THE BAZOOKA

While I was playing truant and rambling around the countryside I acquired some powerful banger fireworks. They were called Crow-scarer's and the local farmer called Mr Jim Tice hung them on burning ropes. As the ropes slowly burnt, it ignited the firework which exploded with a loud bang and scared the crows and pigeons. I found they were very powerful, fo example I found they could blow a heavy metal dustbin lid higher than our house.

I had spent a lot of time with the soldiers that had been billeted in our village and I owned a 4.10 shotgun and a .22 rifle until I lost them when our guest house called Homefields in Runfold. burnt down on the 4th February 1950

There is a Sand quarry there now. Apparently my father was made bankrupt on the 9th of February 1951. I learnt this fact in February of 2016.

It was in 1950 that I decided to build a Bazooka which was a term used by the military for an early rocket launcher which they fired from resting on the shoulder. I obtained an inch diameter galvanized water pipe that was about five feet long from my grandfather. He was a plumber and blacksmith. I had watched him put a thread on pipes so I did that and closed off one end. Then I acquired some roofing nails, these nails had one inch wide heads and they fitted perfectly into the barrel, also they were about three inches long and heavy. I lit a firework and dropped it in the pipe followed by a nail. Then having placed it on my shoulder and aimed it fired, I did this a few times. But I could not see where the nails were going to.

My uncle came across to me in the Café car park and asked what I was doing. He was only two years older than me; he then volunteered to get behind a roofing sheet of galvanized iron while I shot at it. He would tell me if it hit the iron. Now bear in mind this was not thin tin, this was thick and heavy stuff. He got behind it and I walked about fifty yards away. I loaded aimed and fired; I never heard a clang of metal hitting metal. I walked over to where my uncle was still squatting looking at a hole in the metal The nail had gone sideways clean through the metal! It was a good job that he had sat down as it had passed very closely over his head. It would have killed him had it hit him.

I continued firing my bazooka until one day it fired prematurely and skinned my finger as I was loading the nail. I fared better than the boy that lived in the Jolly Farmer Pub as he blew some fingers off with an explosive made from some farm fertilizer. I was very happy to hear about that as a short time previously he had thrown half a house brick at me because I was sitting on his parents pub wall and it knocked one of my front teeth out It was justice I thought.

I met Mr Jim Tice in September (2012) when he purchased my book Dunce or Dyslexic and then by chance met his sister Monica Jones. I told them both about their fireworks and my bazooka. You can see Mr Tice's farm machinery at The Rural Life Centre. This is the largest countryside museum in the south of England.

BUCKET BOY

We lived in a house in nineteen forty three
No electric light, inside toilet, bath or TV
Daddy, Mummy, Midge, Nita, Storm, Gale and
me, I was called Bucket boy, why? You will see

We had an outdoor toilet called a Bog, or Loo
At night we used a bucket, to pee, No poo!
My elder sister with wicked grin, and look of glee
Would fill the bucket over the very top with wee

So much so, it was above the edge, the lip
I had to carry it down the stairs, dare not trip
How could that be, so high? Her action's so low.
Above the bucket's edge, surface tension, now I
know

Bath time was not much fun, you will laugh.
Seven of us, one five foot long, tin bath
Boiling water from a kettle, you jumped out fast
When deeper dirtier hotter, dad was always last

Shallow water, baby in first, out quick
Tilley Paraffin lamps to pump, trim the wick
Candles on the way to bed, upstairs no coal fire
Un-heated bedrooms, cold starched sheets, dire

My bedroom wall was lined with Hop Bag
sacking
Mum had glued wallpaper with flour, mice kept
snacking
We even had a TV Ariel on the roof, it was false,
a fake
We did not have a set. It was for the neighbour's
sake

I had a healthy, reasonably happy childhood
Mum was an angel, and dad like Robin Hood
Mum didn't understand and paddled my bum
I was dyslexic and a slow learner, not dumb.

The House was the Toll House at Runfold.

THE BLACK WATCH

Soldiers had been in requisitioned Victorian
houses throughout the war in our village called
Runfold. Twenty roomed mansions on big
estates, they were playgrounds for my-self and
my friend Roy, the year was 1944. These
properties had gardens full of exotic plants and
trees. The house ceilings were twelve feet high
and full of ornament, plaster patterns, rooms
were huge, twenty by thirty feet wide. It did feel
like heaven, it nearly was.

I admired Black Watch Badges on their beret
with a red plume of feathers. We collected Army
stuff, most given, some found Badges were hard
to obtain, Roy wanted a bayonet.

Thinking the Scottish troops were all on parade
We walked through the imposing mahogany
doors. Up curving stairs with carved rampant
lions, handmade

A room, kit laid out with the kilts and finery.
Sash windows wide open, a warm summer day
Badge, for plucking, bayonet for Roy's armoury

A kilted apparition appeared, bayonet fixed
With bayonet pointed at me, he charged,
screaming a curse, I am transfixed

Full of fright and too small to fight
I turned to flight and dived head first out the
window. I suppose that was not very bright

Landing in a dense bush, I lay taking stock
A fall of eighteen feet, the sergeant appeared at
the window, in a state of shock

He never spoke; I rolled off that bush and ran
away

Next day there was a knock on our house door,
There stood the soldier; he asked if I was okay

When mother opened the door that sunny day
He spoke to Mum in a funny way
Mother told me quietly to "Go away."

Demobilization for the troops. 1945, end of strife
It was my fault she went with that Scot
to Scotland. Auchtermuchty in Fife.

She came back, years later to my dad
I enjoyed having a mum, a few more years
She left again after three more kids were had

Leaving the Army, I bought the café from my
father
My mother had remarried, my father died
I did not serve; dyslexia puts me in a lather

Forty years go by, then on a bright summer day
I was serving in the busy café. In the doorway he
stood, I knew it was him straight away

"You don't know me," he said, looking harried
"I do, you're the Scot from Auchtermuchty,
"Your mother around ?" "Yes, remarried,"

I said, "Wait a minute," as he disappeared
My mother would have loved to see him .Within
a minute, he had gone. That was weird.

Note.
My mother was very upset to find she had
missed the opportunity to see him, we never
heard or saw him again. I never learnt his
surname; was the visit by a ghost?

Mother said life in a Scottish croft was too hard
and remote. I tried to find him through various
Associations but was unsuccessful.

SWEET AND SOUR

Mother told me
Girls are nice
They are made of
Sugar and spice

Boys are always fighting
They are very bad
Play football, get dirty
Get sweaty, like your Dad

Girls are cuddly, soft
They look pretty in pink
Like dolls and furry things
Boys don't wash, like to stink

Girls, if they listen to mother
Learn to play sweet, soft & shy
To convince men of their need
For expensive things to buy

I asked, Mum can I have a dress
I was not at all, soft and shy
Wanted to be a girl to miss the war
Looked so cute, in pink, Oh my

Then I learnt about child birth
I had thought women had it made
A bitter-sweet pill to swallow for me
It made my jealousy of girls fade.

Note.
I was probably about ten years of age and knew
that men had to go to war. Women stayed at
home, and it seemed that they had a better deal
in life. My mother dressed me up one day and
took a photograph of me, after a few hours I
hated it and decided to be all male.

THE TELEGRAM

Devised to pass information quickly
To out-perform pigeon and pony express
The telephone was too informal
Questions could be asked, more distress

Letters were too slow for business
Not many people had a telephone
Business used them, they were quick
Before the newspapers hit the home

There was joy in the message of a birth
And pleasure to get a wedding invitation
Fear of receiving the OHMS telegram
And then the opening of it, in trepidation

With his pillbox hat, blood red jacket
Jaunty, happy delivery man said
Telegram Ma'am. It read John Doe,
Your son injured in action. Now dead

Telegrams were used in those days,
it made me think of the awful times
during the war when families received
those short sharp, to the point messages.

TELLING THE TRUTH

Son that was a fib you told!
Do not tell porky-pies, for telling
Lies, I'll smack you, for fibs, a scold."

Later a policeman visited my dad
And talked about this and that
A quiet chat, is what they had

After he had gone, I ask, why?
I heard you lie to that nice man
Be quiet, or I will make you cry;

But you told me, never to lie
Ah, you see there is a difference
Sometimes you have to, to get by

People get upset, when you tell the truth
Sometimes using a white lie helps to calm,
stops them being awkward or uncouth

Avoids hurt feelings, or appearing weak
So then a little fib called a white lie
it enables you to elaborate, so to speak

Perhaps it is best, to alter truth, to lie
To your husband, wife or child to calm
And soothe. That is a called a porky-pie

THE GUN.

About 1948/my father purchased a large Victorian house called Homefields, It was situate at Whiteways corner in Runfold near Farnham Surrey. It had been requisitioned by the Army for the duration of the war. I knew it well, having played there for years when the Canadian soldiers were there. I must admit that I played truant and spent my afternoons watching very interesting films in their cinema. They used to feed me and get me to try some of their assault courses, even climbing down a rope from the third floor. No safety line. Health and Safety would have a fit these days.

At the end of the War there had been Italian then German prisoners of war at this house. There had been no bars or barbed wire to keep them there. Many Italians stayed after the war and worked on the farms. Some became successful localbusiness men. I found the Germans very interesting and playful. They carved wooden toys; one which they gave to me was like a ping pong bat with four little chicken on it, when you swung the ball hanging below the bat the chicken pecked the bat in rotation.

After the war, one of the Germans stayed and worked for my father for a while, his name sounded like Kinter Fisher but I suspect it might have been spelt Gunter Fisher.

When he returned home my eldest sister corresponded with him but he was on the wrong side of Berlin and the authorities stopped him writing.

I digressed from the story of the gun but not too far because it was a 9mm German automatic pistol, First I will tell you a little more about our house, it was very big, twenty one rooms. It was situated approximately four hundred yards from the road. At the rear there was a large brick building about fifty feet long by thirty feet wide. Originally it was built to grow grapes. At the end was a modern metal double door. In the war the Canadian soldiers made it into a cinema. My father was converting this house into a hotel mainly for lorry drivers and cyclists. The cyclists used to race to Alton and back a distance of thirty miles. It was named The Green's Guest House.

I was now fifteen years of age. Our village milkman who had already taught me to ride his Cotton water cooled motorbike, and that was on the A31 trunk road without Tax and Insurance.

Then one day he showed me a gun that he had acquired, I already had a .410 shotgun and a .22 rifle for shooting rabbits. He offered the pistol for a fiver (£5), a bargain, so I bought it. A deal was done. I was getting pocket money for cleaning in my father's café, mainly horrible jobs like cleaning the toilets. I also had to look after the paraffin lamps in the hotel.

It was a German automatic 9mm pistol; I do not remember the name. It was in perfect condition, like new; there were two boxes of 9mm copper jacket bullets. Next day was Sunday, I went down the Sand quarry next to the house and fired the gun at steel oil barrels, empty ones of course, I was not a vandal! I was amazed when I saw that the bullet went round the fifty gallon oil barrel like a tin-opener.

Returning to the house I showed the gun to my younger brother. We went into the large brick building at the rear of the house, the old greenhouse, there three brick walls and the east side was glass. I told him that the bullet would go through the metal door; we were standing in the middle of the room about five feet from the rear wall by the side door. I fired. A tremendous noise reverberated but was overshadowed by a zing-zing-zing. There was a second of silence then my eldest sister said "What are you doing?" She had stepped through the door as I fired. The bullet hit the stanchion of the door then ricocheted round the walls passing behind all three of us. I dismantled the gun cleaned it then hid it in my room.

A few days later my mother looked like a Panda bear, she had two black eyes. She then locked herself away in her bedroom for two days; my father had hit her for some reason. Life appeared to be relatively normal for a while. Mother running the hotel while my father his café a mile down the road. There was no electricity in the hotel, it was one of my jobs to light the paraffin lamps and place them in the windows to attract customers. When my mother had black eyes, which was more than once, she followed behind me blowing the lamps out. I couldn't get into trouble because I had lit them

One day when everything appeared peaceful. It was afternoon and there were no clients around. A large man strode in, he did not just walk. He had arrogance in his demeanour. He was powerfully built; probably six foot tall, a black patch over one eye, I think it was his right eye. He entered the kitchen where my mother greeted him, "Hallo Stanley," she said, I stood watching from the open doorway, Stanley just said "Where's Alf?" Mum said "I don't know,"

Stanley without a word or moment's hesitation swept his arm down a shelf full of mugs, sending them crashing to the quarry tiled floor. He repeated "Where's Alf?" Another "I don't know." A line of new dinner plates joined the heap on the floor with a crash and tinkle that echoed around the house, more so because there was a scarcity of carpets. A third time he asked and then a cupboard in the kitchen opened and my father came out. I was shocked, ashamed that my father, who was so aggressive to my mother and to others, had hidden like a child in a cupboard. I was told to disappear.

A few days later my mother looked like a Panda again, with two black eyes. She then locked herself away in her bedroom for two days; my father had hit her again for some reason.

Shortly after this my treasured pistol disappeared, I asked my mother about it, she said she had found and it and thrown it away, I did not believe her and went to my father saying, "Dad mum's got my gun." What gun he asked. "My 9mm automatic pistol," I replied. He stiffened; his face went white. Rushing to the house he asked my mother about it, she told him she had thrown it away, I don't think he believed her either for he did not work for nearly three days while he searched the house.

Remember there were 21 rooms, 5 garages, a Cellar of 5 rooms a flat and outhouses, in the end he found it. Of course it was confiscated again; I knew he would keep it for his protection.

AUTUMNAL THOUGHTS

I was five, Mother dragged me crying, to school
Teachers did not understand dyslexia
I was called a fool
After entering the Victorian buildings hall
I saw four posters on the schoolroom wall

Transfixed by the colours across the board
I stared at the autumn scene that I just adored
In beautiful chromolithograph colours
I forgot all about, those three others

Seventy years on, I still enjoy autumn colour
My love of life and life in England is no duller
Myriad shades of green and yellow, spots of red
Interspersed with brown, of trees now dead

Shafts of sunlight, through the trees does filter
Shining on Birch trees with their subtle silver
Golden leaves showering down upon your head
Fallen leaves, a mulch to put the seeds to bed

Teacher gave me a Sand-Box to write in then
It was 1939. I had already used a fountain pen
I learnt to type when aged seventy four
Enabling me to overcome difficulties I'd met
before

It is computer spellcheck that enables me
To write and tell you, what I feel and see
I am not a poet to be remembered in perpetuity
Just writing, fills me with fun and sense of glee

Notes.
Sand-Box was a shallow tray, with a layer of
sand. The pupil wrote in the sand with their
finger a letter or figure then shook the tray to
level the sand for the next letter or word.

Teachers did not understand Dyslexia in those
days.
Dyscalculia is a difficulty in making arithmetical
calculations.

ALF'S CAFÉ IN THE 1950s

This new building was mainly constructed from the remains of the Homefield Guest house which was destroyed by a fire. The steel 'A' frames that support the roof were from the large greenhouse at the back of that fantastic house. You can see the Hop poles in the background.

The Café closed in 1994 due to the A31 being diverted to the north of the village. They now sell products for animals.at this property

HOMEFIELD in 1921

A photo of 'Homefield' dated 1921.This was one of the large and beautiful Victorian houses that housed the troops and later prisoners of war. The building at the back of the house was the 'Orangery' that the Canadian soldiers converted to a cinema. When I was aged between 10 and 11yrs old I was able to watch the latest American films when skipping school.

This house when constructed had its own electricity plant; a laundry with Steam heated drying racks. The house had radiators that were steam heated. Toilets on the ground and 1st floor (but not in the servants quarters on the top floor.) There were septic tanks. The Rainwater was collected in huge tanks on each corner of the building. This supplied a fountain and a curving man-made river on the north-east side of the garden.

Note. Of the above list only the toilets worked when my father purchased the house after the war.

Now think that this was at a time that most of the houses in Runfold had outside bucket toilets, No electricity, No gas, and a lot had dirt floors

THAT IS THE END.

Well it is the end of my war stories. This little book has made me reminisce about my childhood and it has been very interesting. I have found that by walking round the Rural Life Centre at Tilford and viewing the old machinery and workshops, it has re-awakened memories that had disappeared from my mind.

RURAL LIFE CENTRE

Reeds Road (off the A287) Tilford, Farnham, Surrey, GU10 2DL 01252 795571
 www.rural-life.org.uk

BOOKS BY THE SAME AUTHOR.

DUNCE OR DYSLEXIC

By Simpleton (pseudonym for Bernard Green) A Biography. He opened the first Skydiving School in England. He was also co-founder of the British Parachute Association and first secretary. Later he became a commercial Balloon pilot.

This book is also available as a talking book for the blind and partially sighted. To contact the RNIB, call the Helpline on 0303 123 9999 or email helpline@rnib.org.uk to sign up or find out more information.

Note. This is for adult reading.

403 Pages. ISBN Number 978-0-9576042-0-9
£14.99

PARACHUTES, POEMS & POLEMICS
By B.A.N.Green.

The cover was the poster for British Skydiving Ltd. This book covers early parachuting and skydiving in the UK. He also covers a range of subjects in his poems such as Nature, War, Environment, People, Politics and Immigration.

Note. There are some poems and stories that are only suitable for adult reading.

312 Pages. ISBN Number 978-0-9576042-4-7
£7.99

BUILDING THE KHUFU PYRAMID-SHEDDING NEW LIGHT.
By B.A.N.Green.

The author built a small pyramid of scaffolding to prove the concept to Professor Menno P. Gerkema of the Department of Chronobiology and the Department of Science and Society, University of Groningen, the Netherlands.

31Pages. ISBN Number 978-0-9576042-0-9
Price-£4-99.

MY WIFE & CANCER.
By B.A.N.Green.

A story of the mental trauma and difficulties met by the patient that has been diagnosed with cancer. And the stress imposed on their partners. There is no attempt to write about treatment. This is not a sad book.

192 Pages. ISBN Number 978-0-9576042-5-4
Price-£6-99 £1 of the price will be donated to the Fountain Centre at the Guildford Hospital.

SPIES IN VUNGTAU 1915-1920
By B.A.N.Green.

In 1987 the author of this book, purchased a box of 200 Victorian Glass Slides, there were no titles or written history with them so he put them in his loft and forgot them. In 2017 on retirement he examined them and found they were 100years old. Not only that they were exciting photographs of events in Cochin-china and Annam (Vietnam). The photos are related to events in the 1st World War.

158 Pages. ISBN Number 978-0-9576042-9-2
Price -£10.00

All of my books are to be found on Amazon Kindle e Books.
www.amazon.com

The email address for all hard copy book sales is- **berniegreen@live.co.uk**

Hard copy book prices are plus postage.

TO BE PUBLISHED.

ZEPPELINS THAT BOMBED LONDON

This book is not just about the bombing of London, but also the difficulties the Lord Mayor of London (Sir Charles Wakefield) had with the Government and the War Department.
This concerned the defence of London, the Anti-aircraft Gunners and the Searchlight teams.

It also points out the class distinction that was made between the Royal Flying Corps and the Army Gunners.

Graham Spicer who is an archivist helped me in the research and formatting of this book.